Sarah´s little book of Healing

RACHEL GOODWIN

ISBN:9798681628132

CONTENTS

ACKNOWLEDGMENTS

I would like to thank my Mum, Patricia Kennedy, whose passing in 1996 started this whole journey… I'd also like to thank Louise Keoghan for being a constant source of support, inspiration & encouragement for my Sarah work. And to all of the people who have supported my work over the years, thank you – you have made it possible for me to keep doing what I do.
Thank you to my husband, Thomas, who has supported me in doing all of my spiritual work and has understood why I need to do it, and lastly to Sarah, who came into my life in 2005, and has helped me reach places inside myself that no-one else could have reached!!

INTRODUCTION: SARAH'S LITTLE BOOK OF HEALING

In this book the Divine is given different terms, God, Goddess, but please use any term instead of these that you like to use. All parts highlighted in italics are channeled words from Sarah.

Healing is a process that we're constantly going through. Our bodies know how to heal themselves. When you cut your finger, you don't need to do anything, or tell your skin how to heal the wound. We are taught to optimise this healing process by staying in the best condition that we can, by looking after ourselves physically, mentally, emotionally and spiritually.

In the same way, our souls know how to heal ourselves spiritually, and by giving ourselves the right conditions and environment, our souls can achieve great feats of healing, whether it is in our relationships, jobs, finances, our wellbeing, our health and so on.

Sarah is a powerful ally to assist us in our healing process as we walk our path into the New Age of Aquarius. Her energy as an Ascended Master acts as a catalyst for evolutionary change, helping us move ourselves and our lives into the energy of the New Age of Aquarius. This is a great work for each of us. We are clearing many things, our past lives and perhaps an even greater work of clearing is that of our ancestral lines. The Divine Feminine energy is being resurrected in western culture, and is restoring to us our healing and intuitive abilities; many are learning to develop their natural psychic and spiritual gifts that are an integral part of our humanity.

We are moving into the New Age or Age of Aquarius; a time of balance and harmony. Sarah comes in female form, to show us that equally as the son of God came to save us, now the daughter comes, to teach us how we can heal ourselves, & create from a place of wholeness. In the archetype of the Christ Sarah, the female form is honoured as sacred, (something which we have been lacking in Western culture), born again in a new story of the Holy Family. In Tau Malachi's beautiful book 'The Gospel of St. Mary Magdalene' he writes,

"Thus according to the Sophian Tradition, St. Mary Magdalene is said to be the soul mate of Lord Yeshua and becomes his closest disciple. Yet more than a disciple, she is said to be his wife & consort, co-equal & co-enlightened with him, and she is a co-preacher of the Gospel. In him, Christ the Logos (word) is embodied and, in her, Christ the Sophia (Wisdom) is embodied. Through their union in the mystery of hieros gamos (the sacred marriage), the Divine fullness of the Christos is revealed."

In this story of Jesus & Mary Magdalene we can find equality, honour and dignity for women as well as for men; & the blueprint of the profound metaphysical significance contained within the sacred marriage. These ideas and stories are arising now in our culture because they reflect something true and real that is occurring on the inner planes; we are being prepared for our own inner sacred marriage. And as we read & hear these stories something deep within us responds, and we know they speak a truth to us; they also help the process of the sacred marriage to be facilitated within ourselves. From that place of the Divine fullness within us will the Age of Aquarius be created, and Sarah, (who is the result of that sacred marriage) has come to help us make that happen.

In the first four chapters of this book, Sarah's healing process has been broken down into parts. These are processes that have been given to me & developed in the years that I have worked with Sarah's guidance & healing energy. The steps as they are laid out are for easy use, but they can be interchanged or used separately. For 'simple' issues, you can use these as steps in a therapeutic exercise which you could complete within an hour or so. For more 'difficult' or larger issues, you can work with each of these processes, one week at a time. (There are lists in the appendix that show suggested break downs of the steps.)

The last 3 chapters of the book are dedicated to some of the channelings on love & healing that Sarah has brought through over the years. More than the words themselves and the teachings, you will receive light and key/grail codes through Sarah's energy which are embedded in the channelings themselves.

Healing can be seen as a way of bringing down higher energies or even of bringing God to bear on a situation or issue. Instead of seeing the difficulties & the pain that we experience in our lives as a problem, we can work to shift our perspective & see them as an opportunity which say to us 'here, we need the healing here'. Then we can connect to the divine part of ourselves/ our soul, or higher self to bring through the healing and wisdom which is needed. It is our difficulties and problems that keep us moving towards the Divine, & we become more light and connect to more of our divinity in ourSelves.

The idea of bringing down energies or of 'inviting something in' is a central concept to working with Sarah's energy. Sarah integrates; she brings things together & provides the framework for our resistances to dissolve. Sarah holds the energy of unity consciousness, of oneness; in her there is no separation. This is a great mystery & as a concept it is not easily explained in our world of polarity. The alchemists of medieval times were fascinated by the synthesis of opposites and the hieros gamos (sacred marriage). Jung's last book which he took 10 years to write, 'Mysterium Coniunctionis – an inquiry into the separation and synthesis of psychic opposites in Alchemy' is devoted to writing about this very thing, 'The coniunctio is the uniting of separating qualities... The factors which come together in the coniuncto are conceived as opposites, either confronting one another in enmity or attracting one another in love.' (Jung 1963)

When Sarah's presence is with us, those things within us that are opposite & separated - male/female, hate/love, light/dark and heaven/earth can unite. She helps us access what is within us as potential; because this energy of unity is already there deep inside us. The synthesis of opposites is for the mind a challenging affair, nevertheless we can access & utilise Sarah's integrative & healing effect simply by asking her for her help. Inviting Sarah to accompany us gives us a powerful tool to progress on our spiritual journey.

All of the exercises in this book have been used extensively for 1:1 sessions, in groups and workshops, and for online 3 week healing courses working with Sarah's energies. In the years that I have worked with Sarah's energy, I have experienced profound and deep changes that have been directly brought about by calling in Sarah. For example, when I did a 'cutting away' chant (see meditation links in the appendix) to Sarah for 3 weeks, a relationship of 4 years suddenly came to an end, because Sarah cut the karmic links between me and this person; due to our past life happenings this relationship had caused me no end of guilt and low self-esteem. It was entirely unexpected and I was expecting just the guilt and self-esteem to be cut away, rather than the actual relationship, however when our energy changes and shifts, our lives change and shift in unison.

Sarah is stepping forward now, as an Ascended Master teacher for the Age of Aquarius. Many of us feel that we are in momentous times in the evolution of the human race. We are moving into a higher vibration and are evolving a new way of how we function in relation to our souls/ higher selves, which is mirrored by changes in our energy bodies. We are the pioneers of this, and are breaking new ground. However each of us isn't achieving this singlehandedly. It is the work of the Divine to 'make this so', and we are all involved in our own unique & perfect way, all of playing our own unique & perfect part. Sarah is here to help us with this change, & give us her support. She is offering to walk by our sides, shining her light down upon our path so we may benefit from her presence.

When we work with Sarah's energy, we **are** pioneers, as she is helping us to create something new. We are giving birth to new ways of being, directly from the light within us in our hearts & souls. And we can find new solutions to old problems. By inviting the dark into the light, and the light into the dark, the fullness of the divinity within us is born.

'I am Sarah' channeling

"Welcome all.

I am the Ascended Lady Master Sarah. She who was born to the Master Jesus and The Magdalena, Mary Magdalene.

I have come to tell you of my news, that I am returned here once again, not in physical form, but through conduits, sources of energy, through the hearts of mankind, my light, my power is being given birth to on earth. This birth is happening as we speak, as you read these words, my love, my light, the power that I represent is manifesting onto the physical planes.

These are mysteries which are the Divine's gift to you, mankind has paid heed to the call; lightworkers across the planet have worked and toiled, struggled and persevered, lifted their hearts and minds in love and joy and so the vibrational energy of the collective consciousness of humanity, and of the earth has risen enough that my arrival has been achieved.

But first, let me explain to you some of what this means.

My energy represents the fusion of and perfect balance between the Christ energy (male) and the Magdalene flame (female). I am these two energies combined to create a third and perfectly balanced, harmonious energy.

This energy has not been present on the earth plane before this moment. In my lifetime, I held the energy, which was born, as I was from the sacred union between my parents. I was the receptacle for this perfect power, but was simply a vessel to hold the power, as it was not the time for this energy to be birthed upon the world.

Since that time, I have held the imprint of the energy within my soul's pattern, so that one day, when the conditions had been sufficiently met, and all was in place, mankind and all of physical manifestation could be impregnated with this awesome power, through me, the conduit for this power.

This is my work then, to birth this power across the earth, as the Master Jesus held the Christ flame and my mother, Mary Magdalene birthed the Magdalene flame, so I hold my power, which is symbolised by my flame and I bring it to you, to all of physical manifestation. The timing of this birthing has been designed to coincide with the coming of the Age of Aquarius, and is indeed the energy which will bring about the Age of Aquarius. This power which is being gifted to you is no small thing! Being gifted to you indeed it is, because now it is present upon the earth plane, it is present upon the earth grid, and so is freely available to all with intent to use it.

I have come to help you achieve many things. If it helps you feel more comfortable, you could think of my existence as a metaphor for the perfect joining of two polarities to create a third. No-one can prove of whether or not I ever existed upon the earth, but as a concept of an energy borne from the sacred union of the Divine Masculine and the Divine Feminine, I am most believable! I represent the sacred Divinity which is within each of us. I am the awesome power of my Father, and the awesome love of my Mother combined to make a third most incredible power.

Open your hearts and breathe me in, I am there, already, lying dormant, waiting to be awakened. My energy can be seen as the bright green of nature, the colour of spring, new leaves growing on the branches, abundant growth. My father, performed many miracles. I am here to light up your hearts so you can perform those miracles yourself. Remember who you are!

You are the Divine made manifest, the divine clothed in the wonders of matter. It is time to awaken, time to remember; you are not the consciousness of your body and your mind, they are the physical manifestation of you. Each of you is the Divine, birthed into manifestation, given individual consciousness. I have come to help you remember what you already know, to empower you to be the perfect and divine beings that you are. The whole world, the whole universe has been waiting for this moment, and now it is here. I have come, I have come, I am here, I am here. A messenger for the Divine, who wishes for it to be known that the time has come for a message of hope and joy to be spread across the earth.

All is well, all is well, all is well. My power, my light, my love, will grow exponentially upon the earth in the years to come. If you like, you could liken me to the power of Spring, for I have come to usher in a new era, a new beginning not just for humankind but for all of existence. I am new beginnings, new hopes; my power will seem at first to grow slowly but this is because in reality, enormous surges of power will be required to overcome the inertia of the old, of what has been, and help it to flow in a new way, to seek out new pathways.

You can, if you wish, help my flow to gather pace by calling on me, bringing my energy into you, breathing it into you and sending it out to the world, wherever you feel

.

it has need. Or simply calling on me, and grounding me into the earth. And of course you can call on me to manifest in your own life.

In wishing to empower you to be the perfect and divine beings that you are, my energy will help you grow ever towards your highest potential, your greatest possible brilliance at any given moment, your greatest capacity for love, in all things, from the smallest to the greatest act, thought or feeling. There is much that I have come to teach you, much that I have to give, but for now, let it be enough for me to tell you that I am here, I have come. That I am full of joy and love for humanity and manifest creation.

Let your hearts sing and be proud at what you have achieved through the power of your own free will. I am here because of you! You are bringing about the Age of Aquarius. Jubilations to All!!

May love and blessings shower down upon the New Earth, created anew in each moment. Bright Blessings! Lady Sarah."

1 GETTING READY TO RECEIVE HEALING

It's good to do some preparation to receive healing. Preparation can give us a much better result. If you are planting seeds, it's important to prepare the ground first, clear any weeds or stones that might stop the tender shoots from reaching up through the soil, & improving the soil by making it more nutritious & rich for the seedlings to have the right growing conditions.

When we prepare for healing we want to do similar things with our energy field, removing any blocks and clearing the space so that the healing can occur & putting in good energies to provide the optimum conditions for growth and healing.

Sometimes we haven't been able to achieve our healing goals because of our own resistance. It can be that the universe is ready to give us healing and it is us who are in the way because we're resisting, often unconsciously. This may sound a little crazy, but there are often reasons for this that we will look into a little bit further on.

Sarah's Violet Flame

You can use Sarah's violet flame to prepare you for healing.

To help us untangle any energies or resistance that

surround our issue, we can use healing tools, such as Sarah's violet flame. This is an energy which she works with, and we can call on this before doing any healing work. Sarah's violet flame will help you prepare the way.

"My violet flame will allow you to transform and transmute the darker energies of your life into those that will help you live in accordance with your divinity. These areas will be in vibrational resonance with the New Earth and the New Age of Aquarius and allow you to live in harmony with and have your consciousness in the higher dimensions"

The violet flame is known for transmuting and transforming negative energies into positive energies, many systems of healing & even mystery schools work with the violet flame and it is an energy that is very close to the energy of creation. Since creation occurred, it has never stopped changing, & our universe is in a constant process of change and evolution. It is the natural course of events, for life to constantly move and change, & if things have become a little stuck or rigid, the violet flame can help the flow return to its natural state, and can allow your issue or situation to move onto its next state of natural growth.

Sarah has her own vibration of violet flame which you can call on. It is the essence of evolutionary change for the Age of Aquarius and will help your process happen 'under grace and in perfect ways' to its greatest potential. It will help you dissolve any resistance you have to creating what you want in your life, & also help you become conscious of those issues during the healing process. It will also help you to create that which is in accordance with the Divine Will and in vibrational alignment with the Age of Aquarius.

Sarah's violet flame comes to cleanse us of what no longer serves us, specifically so we are ready to move into the Age of Aquarius. Part of our 'destiny' in the New Age is to learn how to create from our deepest hearts desires, which is to create from the centre of ourselves/ our Divinity. In the Gospel of St. Mary Magdalene (Malachi, 2006), it is said "God...has entered in through the image of the Daughter. The light entered (with the son) but was too bright, and so now the fire comes to purify so that all might be sanctified to receive the True Light." Our True Light is the Divine Spark which exists at the centre of being, and Sarah is the guide who shows us the way; her violet flame clears the way so we can see the path.

You can use Sarah's violet flame exercise (see this at the end of the chapter) before you start any healing work. You could say something like, 'I call upon Sarah and her violet flame to help me transform & transmute all negative & inappropriate energies, beliefs, thoughts & emotions within and around me that are connected to my (example) abundance & prosperity & I ask that this occurs through divine grace & in a perfect way. I give thanks for all of your help & assistance Sarah in these matters. Amen/ So may it be.'

You can also connect to Sarah's violet flame by looking at the picture of Sarah on the website. (see on line resources at the end of the book) Around Sarah's head is a halo of her violet flame (picture prints are also available on my website)

Quick ways of using the Violet flame

- Say 'I call upon Sarah's violet flame to be around me and all through me.'
- Picture, imagine or simply know that the violet flame is surrounding you, and infusing you.
- If it is a situation that you want to transform, picture the situation in your mind's eye and put the violet flame through it (or think through each aspect & detail of the situation, repeatedly saying 'Sarah's violet flame flows through this')
- If you have a health issue that you need to heal, breathe Sarah's violet flame up through the earth and into your feet, and into the specific area
- For a longer version, do a violet flame meditation (you can see a suggested meditation at the end of this chapter)

St. Germaine and Lady Portia are the keepers of the violet flame, although there are aspects of the violet ray which are also overseen by other Ascended Master & Angels. If you connect strongly with this energy and would like to know more, look at 'Violet flame, to heal body, mind & soul' by Elizabeth Clare Prophet.

What is it you want to heal and why?

As a first step, get really clear on what it is you want to heal and why, & what you want the outcome to be. For example, you might want to heal your issues around relationships because you want to have closeness and intimacy by attracting a loving partner. Make it very clear in your mind what you want the outcome to be. Write down and imagine what that outcome would look like, feel like, imagining as many details as you possibly can.

For example, what would be different about you if you had a loving partner? What would that 'you' sound like when they were talking to others, what would they hold themselves like & what would that 'you' feel like on a day to day basis?

Part of you is often resistant to change

It is often a natural part of our ego's process that it is fearful of change. We feel more comfortable with what we know already, (& some of us more than others!!) as it likes to know what is going on, and it can feel uncomfortable stepping into the unknown. For example, If I am going into something new, like starting a course, or having an initiation and I feel particularly anxious/ fearful or even just suddenly and for no particular reason feel extremely ambivalent about going (do I really have the time, sigh, I'm so tired/ busy) then I take it as a good sign that what I'm about to do is going to be a powerful thing for me **because** I'm throwing up resistance against it. In my experience, the more something is going to be life changing for me, the more resistance I throw up against it. Developing our intuition and other psychic senses is very helpful in cases like this, as it can keep us steered on the right path, even when our more earthly selves are having all the little doubts and fears that we do!

So it could be that there is part of you that is resistant to this change, even though it is something you consciously want; often parts of ourselves are trying to protect us & are fearful or doubtful and this may have sabotaged the healing of this up until now. Or it may be that you have just become aware of your healing issue, and that it feels rather big and you would like some support with it. These parts often need a bit of extra help and support as part of the healing process, and working with the violet flame will help 'soften up' these resistances and gently expose what worries, fears or doubts you might have that need to be brought into the light of day. You might think of using the violet flame as pouring a bit of water on the hard-baked mud to make it soft enough to dig into it.

For example, as you work with the violet flame, you might start to become aware that a part of you feels that because of bad experiences in the past (this life, childhood, or past life issues) then it is safer for you to be alone, and in an effort to protect you from others, this part of you keeps all potential partners at a distance. Additionally, there might be a part of you that has inherited beliefs from your ancestral line that do not work well with having an intimate relationship! Beliefs can come down the ancestral line, sometimes they have been travelling along for generations, and you can often receive them whole as you're born into this line. These beliefs can be quite difficult to get conscious of because they've always been there, but once you do become aware of them, they can be quite easy to shift.

Life as Daily Therapy

When you start to work with Sarah's violet flame, be aware of what things come up for you in your daily life, and notice the little things. Often you are being given a great deal of information in the way you respond to other people & the feelings they bring up in you, and in the words that other people speak to you, and the situations and happenings that you observe throughout the day.

If you are working with, for example, your 'healing relationships' goal & start to do the violet flame exercises, you could (in your everyday life) have an experience of seeing someone else who ever so subtly keeps people at arm's length, maybe by always choosing partners who will let them down, and have a realisation that this is exactly what YOU do. Often we come across these kind of experiences as mirrors for our own lives, & we notice them right at the moment that we are ready to SEE what is going on in our own. Be particularly aware for any situations involving other people that particularly upset or irritate you; often such situations are a gold mine, reflecting back to us a wealth of information.

When you start to do this work, Sarah is walking by your side, guiding your every step, and nudging you towards the healing and insight you need. She will put people, places and situations in your path that will help you the most. Take everything (even the bits you don't like) as a gift, then ask Sarah in your journaling or daily prayers/ meditations what lessons or meaning it has for you; you could ask 'what do I need to know about this person reacting in such and such a way to me', as things can often reflect things back to us – not for punishment, but as the universe helping us gain insight into all aspects of our being. It could be that the situation of somebody treating you unfairly, when you sit down and contemplate upon it, reveals to you a strong message that you deserve compassion and kindness, and that you get that really clearly in a way that you will no longer accept anything than this from yourself or others. Sometimes when we ask for what we need to know about a situation, it comes to us immediately as information or a realisation. Sometimes it can come a little while later, or in another way.

The universe teaches us through example every day, by the everyday events that go on around us. Start to pay more attention to everything that happens to you and the people around you; the way things play out, what you observe in other people, & what you hear, say and feel.

Life is teaching us all the time and giving us wisdom about what we need to know and how we can heal.

Write down what it is you want to change

Write down what it is you want to change/or have changed in your life. Get in touch fully with everything you want to get rid of. Don't hold yourself back or feel you've got to be positive about it! The reason for this is to make as much as possible of this difficult and negative material conscious, because then we can bring healing into it. This is very 'Sarah' to be with all the difficult & dark bits as well as the positive and light stuff, and then to integrate them – **Sarah integrates**.

Another way of doing this is to draw how these things feel to you. Get some crayons or paints or whatever you have and some paper. Check inside yourself, and notice whether these feelings have a colour, or even an image of what they look like. Draw on the paper what's inside you. Get it all out.

You might also like to try other ways. Get together a group of objects, stones, paper, old recycling, be as creative as you can be, and put them together in a way that symbolizes your inner world. You can collage & write words on the paper as well. Or you might have an object that symbolizes this for, or want to print something out from your computer. Do whatever feels right for you.

Write down the essence of what it is that is wrong in your life right now

After you have allowed yourself to feel as much you can right now, then write down the essence of what it is that's 'wrong'. Staying with the example above, it might be 'my relationships always end in disaster', or 'I can never get close to anyone' or 'I can't trust anyone'. It could be anything in your life, 'I can't seem to earn any money', 'I don't know what to do with my life', 'I'm useless at dealing with problems'. We're not judging here, just being really honest about how we feel. When you've got clear about this, write it down on a piece of paper where you can see it.

Surround this issue with the violet flame

Breathe/ visualise/ have the intent that Sarah's violet flame flows through your issue. In the next chapter we will take what you have written down into Sarah's healing circle.

'How to Pray for Healing' channeling

"There is a trick here, an alchemy to bringing down the higher energies (which also come from the centre of yourSelf) and weaving them into the pain and darkness you experience. The trick is to have the intent/ hope that it should be so (the healing), and then pray to mother/father God/ The Divine & ask God to have it be so.

When you need love, pray for love. When you need compassion and understanding, pray for compassion & understanding. If you need fear and hate removed from a relationship you are in, pray that it be removed.

Feel the need inside you of what needs to change, and then pray that might be so. Thereafter, watch out for signs and symbols that it is coming true. Expect God to answer your prayer. Also notice any answers or help coming your way; maybe a piece of wisdom you needed to hear, or a course or session that will help you to achieve your goal.

You cannot achieve these things on your own. You can only notice in your conscious awareness what it is that needs to change, what needs to be 'lifted up', and then use that awareness to request the healing that is needed from the Divine. Miracles are not achieved by the ego, but by the God/ Christ consciousness, which is at once 'out there' and also 'within'.

Everything within and without of creation is God/ Goddess, do you think there is anything she cannot achieve?!! Think then, on how possible your little prayers are to God, how achievable!!

Imagine then that God is just waiting for your call; that the Divine itself is hoping and praying that you will ask for this very thing, so it can be given to you. Don't you think God wants you to be full of love, healing, joy, hope, prosperity and all other good things?

To know this in your heart, that God wants all good things for you, is to always have hope then, because you are loved, and if you are loved, then good things will always be found, is that not so?

These simple truths hold the greatest keys to love, joy & happiness.

God is the way, always look to the Divine to provide you with what you need, and never cease in your looking to find the answers to your prayers.

May blessings pour down upon you each and every day, Blessed Be, Blessed Be, Blessed Be. Sarah."

Sarah's Violet Flame Meditation

This is a suggested outline for a meditation, but you can change it to suit your own particular preferences.

- Sit comfortably upon a chair, with your spine straight, or lie down. Take several deep breaths and clear your mind. Call on Sarah's violet flame and draw it up from the earth through the soles of your feet, see, feel, or know that the violet flame has entered you, and draw it up slowly, through your feet, ankles, calves, knees etc, until you have reached your neck. Then call upon the violet flame to flow down through your arms and hands. Finally lift the violet flame up through your head.
- Be as specific or as quick as you wish, i.e., you may wish to give yourself a thorough cleansing, and focus on as many details as you can imagine; each part of the physical body has a vital part to play, and the foundations of bones, marrow, blood, can accumulate negative energy as so can the vital organs, of heart, brain etc.
- Concentrate on any areas where you feel any excess energy, ie, a build-up of tension in the shoulders or a headache, and spend more time working the violet flame through these areas.
- As you are directing the violet flame up from your feet towards your head, you may also wish to direct the violet flame to flow through each of your chakras in turn, again spending more time on particular chakras where you feel or know there is a blockage, or build-up of unwanted energy. If for example, there is a blockage of expression of grief, take extra care taken to work the violet flame through the region of the sacral and heart chakra, as it will help to facilitate the energy of the sorrow and grief to be released,

through crying etc.

- As Sarah's violet flame is coursing through your physical body, it will also be flowing through the etheric counterpart, which lies in the same size and space as your physical body, but exists on a different plane, and is composed of slightly higher vibrations. When you have completed directing the violet flame through your body, state, 'the violet flame is now present in each cell and particle in my physical and etheric body, and is transmuting and transforming all that is negative or inappropriate.'

- After this stage, expand the violet flame from your physical and etheric body, out into all of your energy bodies. There are different layers to the aura, and again you can work through each of these in turn, such as your emotional aura and your mental aura, where thoughts and beliefs are held, paying as much care and attention as you wish. Or you can expand the violet flame in a great 'whoosh', knowing that any negative or inappropriate energies are being transmuted and transformed, having the intent of expanding it right to the very edges of your aura.

- If you are experiencing difficulty in working through a particular energy blockage or problem in your life, which could express itself as a physical illness, a situation or issue or as an emotional dynamic, i.e., being unable to let go of anger, tension, fear and so on, call on Sarah and imagine what needs healing in your mind's eye and ask Sarah to fill it with the transformative power of her violet light. Remember to respect the law of giving and receiving, and to give thanks to those beings that you call upon for assistance, and send them your 'best wishes', by sending them your love, joy, peace etc.

- When you have finished working with the violet flame, feel yourself grounded down through your feet into the earth beneath you and give thanks to Sarah for her help and for her violet flame.

2 CREATING THE HEALING SPACE

When I do 'Sarah' work, I create a space to work in called 'Sarah's healing circle'. This space of Sarah's presence is very grounding, and allows you to become very present. It is the space within which the integrative healing takes place and it is Sarah's power & presence that holds you and all that you are within it.

My experience of being in Sarah's healing circle is one of great depth. I really love being in caves, and it has that feeling of 'deepness' to me that I love in caves. You are also 'held' within her healing circle & it has a chalice like quality. But her healing circle is whatever it is that is good for you. Some people feel very expansive in them, or as if they are high up on a mountain top. It's really different for everyone as you get what you need.

Creating Sarah's Healing Circle

In your mind's eye, imagine that you are sitting within a circle. You can make it somewhere beautiful in nature, somewhere you like to be, or somewhere that you imagine for the first time now. You are perfectly protected sitting in this circle. It is a sacred space & is over and above you (in a three dimensional sphere) and is all around you.

Ask Sarah to come into the circle with you & imagine her sitting there with you. Feel/ see or imagine her presence entering, & as it does, imagine it grounding you & the whole space within the circle & is bringing an energy of fullness/ wholeness to the circle. Sit and breathe this in for a few deep breaths. Say to yourself 'Sarah is with me'.

Talk to Sarah

Talk to Sarah now, as you would if you were sitting with a trusted friend or mentor. Have with you your healing issue that you have written down or drawn etc. As you focus on this, tell her what it is you want to heal & why. Tell her what it is you would like, or what your goal is. Tell her what your fears & doubts are around this healing issue. Tell her everything that you need to tell her right now. Tell her everything that is in your heart. She is listening to you.

Ask Sarah for her help

Ask Sarah to be with you & help you whilst you do this work. Put as much feeling and intent into this as you can; the more you mean it, the more she can help you. She will overlight your path, walk by your side, and give you her presence. This will cause healing and changes to happen to the greatest of your potential, for your highest good & in vibrational resonance with the New Age of Aquarius. Invoking Sarah in this way is a powerful act; keep your eyes and ears open in the days, weeks, and months ahead for Sarah's presence in your life, & be aware of what you notice.

Pray to Sarah with all of your heart

You could say something like this, 'Sarah please help me with this. Please show me what I need to know right now. Please help me understand my situation. Please help me see what I need to see on the path ahead of me. Please help me to receive all the love & healing that I need right now & please bring those people and things into my life that will help me overcome/ heal this situation. Please lead me towards what is real and away from what is unreal. Please teach me how to be with all the things in my life. I ask you to overlight my journey and walk with me on my path until this has been resolved. Thank you Sarah for all of your help in these things, Blessed Be, Amen'

Sarah's Presence

Sarah's presence is a divine energy or archetypal force. She acts as a catalyst & brings about evolutionary change.

"Every time you connect with my presence, every time you think of me, I bring you more into alignment with your own truth. My presence soaks into your very being, altering even the cells and DNA within you. I am that which makes you more of yourself, which is the essence of your soul. Each time you connect with me, a little more of all that is not of the Divine (or of yourSelf) is sloughed off, & falls away. I will take you deeper and deeper into the layers of your being, which of course also takes you higher and higher, as both these things are one and the same (as above so below).
My presence therefore is life altering in this way. As you become more and more yourSelf, you cannot help but make changes in your life. Those things that were there because of expectation, conditioning, avoidance, lack of focus, or whatever it was, have to fall away once you are vibrating with the truth of your soul, they cannot stand to be there any longer."

The Healing Effect of Sarah

Sarah's energy is one of oneness. In Her there is no separation. This is something that that can be felt inside yourself as a divine truth. In working with her energy, I have observed the effect of integration which she manifests. If feels very magnetic, and often I have had the image of Sarah at the centre of a sphere acting as a force towards which everything is magnetised. When we call upon her presence, all of those parts of us that are 'missing' start to travel back towards us pulled back & magnetised towards the centre of the gravitational field which is ourSelf. Sarah is wholeness. She activates our own innate ability for wholeness.

Because she is a Divine Presence, this process of integration which she initiates is overseen by her. It doesn't happen in an accidental, chaotic way, but will occur in a process of divine synchronicity. There is a Hawaii'an expression 'ika pono mea', which means, 'right time, right place, right being' and it describes this process. This is how it happens.

Polarities will unite in the Presence of Sarah

To be in Sarah's Presence is to be on a path of personal & spiritual development. In her all things are in oneness; male & female, dark & light, heaven & earth. In oneness, there is only balance, only harmony; nothing else can be present. She is the result of the sacred marriage, in her there is no separation; the Divine masculine and the Divine feminine have come together in perfect union to create a third energy, something entirely different from the sum of its parts (which are polarity), because it is a seamless energy of unity & oneness. In the history of creation, this unity existed before the polarity and is a more ancient and primal form of the Divine.

When we come into contact with an energy, we begin to resonate with it (just like a tuning fork will create resonance). When we come into contact with Sarah's oneness, something inside us will start to respond in sympathetic resonance, and sing along to the same tune. (Also we have already the seed of oneness within us, in the deepest part of our being) In this way, just being in her energy will have the effect of starting to bring you into balance in your polarities, male & female, right & left brain hemispheres, logic and intuition, dark and light, heaven and earth, the conscious & the unconscious. Whatever is lost or missing in you will start the journey home. Split off parts of your personality, soul fragments which have been lost in past lives, even soul mates , twin flames and soul groups will start to be magnetized towards your path, if they are not there already.

But remember, everything happens in 'ika pono mea', right time, right place, right being. Just as when you build a house, you have to start with the foundations and build upwards before you can put the roof on; the journey back to wholeness, integration and coming 'back home to yourSelf', will happen in Divine order, and you will need to complete each step of the path before you can take the next one. Sarah tells many of us in her messages (me included!), '..take the next step. You don't need to know where it is going, or how it will all end up, just see what is in front of you that you need to do, and do it!' It often happens this way, that when we do take the next step, the next one gets shown to us, and so on and so on. We have to learn to trust that 'God's perfect plan is built upon a rock'!!

This also means that your earthly self and your heavenly

self will be irresistibly drawn together in the presence of Sarah; & when this process finishes completion you will be living as your Higher Self on earth/ as your soul being; which is the goal for all of mankind during the Age of Aquarius. Sarah can help immeasurably with this process. Right now we are unconscious of our divine selves, & yet they are who we are. In oneness, our divinity will know our earthly selves, and we will be consciously aware of & 'know' our divinity with all of the aspects of our earthly being, heart, soul & mind.

Sometimes things just disappear!!

In Sarah's Presence all that is real will be highlighted, for example your true feelings about a situation will be unavoidably clear to you, as if someone was sweeping a marker pen over them so you just can't miss them. In the same way all that is not real is also made clear. This process can take some time, depending on the depth of the realisation you need to have, and the work you have already done.

Sometimes when you invoke Sarah's Presence for an issue, you will find that it is immediately swept away. This is because it was an illusion that you were ready to release. The difficulty was not real, or belonged to someone else's thinking (this could be cultural ideas that you have taken on, or part of your family's thinking, or a partner, friend etc) Or it could be an old fear that you thought you still had, but actually you now find when it disappears in Sarah's presence that you have worked through it. There are many reasons why and this usually becomes clear at the moment the illusion goes.

Completing the Circle

It's good to keep a journal, either after doing your healing exercises and meditations or if you are working more long term, on a daily or weekly basis. There will be things happening where you sense Sarah's presence, that maybe it was her hand that helped bring a certain person into your path, or gave you an inspiration that helped you behave differently in a familiar situation. Make a note of these things, give them attention, and say thank you to Sarah for her help and assistance in your life. At first, you may feel a little unsure whether it was just coincidence, but don't ignore anything, give it all the possibility of doubt that maybe it was Sarah walking with you on your spiritual path. As you do this, and practice looking out for her presence in this way, it will become easier and easier for you to recognise her presence. As you give thanks for what you have received, you open your heart to Sarah and make a space to be given more.

Gratitude is the Key

Know that Sarah is helping you from the moment that you ask, and practice 'an attitude of gratitude'. For many of us, this is a task which starts as a practice, and later develops into true meaning, as we become truly grateful for all the blessings in our lives.

"Blessings are upon you, each and every moment of your life, Blessed Be, Blessed Be, Blessed Be, Sarah."

3 JOURNEYING TO THE CENTRE OF YOURSELF (DISCOVERING YOUR DIVINE IMMANENCE)

Why journey?

It doesn't matter what our situation is, or what we want help with, journeying can always give us some form of assistance. When we set out to journey, we don't know what form the help we receive will come in. It could be insight, resources, wisdom or healing. Even prophecy & how the path will be laid out before us. In the appendix, you can find suggested journeys for working with your dreams, for ancestral healing, and for single session journeys or a longer 3 week process. But you can apply these techniques to anything in your life, whether they are in your inner life or your outer life. So they could equally be, 'why can't I find a job' or 'why is this person annoying me so much', or 'how can I create more abundance in my life?' or 'how can I focus more on my spiritual path?'

These are healing methods which I have developed over a number of years from the guidance that Sarah gave me during healing sessions & they have worked well for myself & many other people.

Taking an Inner Journey

The process of taking this inner journey is one of

allowing; going to the deepest part of our being, we discover the centre of **ourSelves**, and in so doing, we can discover that this feels like a natural, normal part of ourselves. Sarah makes this journey possible, even for those of us who haven't connected this deeply to **ourSelves** before. In her Presence, the bridge between the different parts of ourselves is created & we can cross with ease.

As we practice taking ourselves into this space, & doing this journey to the centre of ourSelves, we find resources there that we never knew existed. From this place, we can find the wisdom and healing that we need. Eventually the practice becomes a way of being, and we find that we have learnt how to live from this place.

During the session, we need to take into the circle and have with us, our 'felt issue'. This is what we did the preliminary work for. Have your words/ writing/ drawing or object with you that encapsulates for you all of the feelings and difficulties you have already evoked. Let the energy of 'all that' be there.

One of Sarah's gifts is to teach us the art of **Allowing**. In Sarah, all things can be. I've often had the experience that as soon as I have connected with her, that I've had an instant realisation about something I feel. This is because we defend ourselves against uncomfortable truths or painful realities. Some of you will have had this experience with a therapist or trusted friend or loved one. It is only when we are in some else's presence that we can face the truth in the situation. This is partly what happens with Sarah; partly it is because we are not alone in her presence, but it is also because her presence dissolves the wall of separation we have (generally unconsciously) built between us and our emotions.

In Sarah's healing circle, we can allow ourselves to **Be** with everything as it is, in all its aspects. This then is what we take with us when we journey to the Centre of ourSelves. At the Centre of our Being, we have access to all the healing that we need. (I once heard these words from Jesus, 'there is no wound so great that it cannot be healed by the love of the Divine Mother.') Our souls are the channel through which this healing is given to us from the Divine. But first of all we have to connect to this wound, and allow it to be there, allow it to be felt. As much of it that can be felt, can be healed.

Sometimes it is insight we need into our situation. A higher/ different perspective can reframe a whole situation for us, so that it is no longer a wound. Sometimes we need healing energy, and our soul can supply this to us in bountiful measures. Sometimes we need both. When you are at the centre of your being, give yourself some time and space to allow whatever you need to come through.

When I started doing healing sessions with Sarah, she gave me this image of a cross within a circle, and I soon discovered that from the centre of this place, & in Sarah's presence, we can access our soul's wisdom and healing. When we journey in our mind's eye & in our intent to the centre of the circle where the cross meets, it takes us to a place deep inside Ourselves, to the Centre of our Being. I have often had the vision of Sarah being at the centre of the circle, in a place of dynamic stillness & peace (a little like the eye of the storm), whilst creation spins around her. This is a metaphor for the archetypal energy that she represents and gives some sense of the power held within that centre.

Part of this healing is to allow your issue to be turned into a healing gift, or an ongoing healing intent. For example, if you have had an issue with trust, whether it is yourself, others or the Universe/ God/ Goddess, your written statement of what was wrong may have been, 'things always go bad for me'. After you have received your healing, the healing gift in this could be the spiritual knowing & truth of 'I am supported in everything that I do, all is well'.

How to journey to the Centre of yourSelf

- From chapter two, you have already placed yourself in Sarah's healing circle & are sitting within her energy. Take some deep breaths and relax your body & your mind. Be with what you want to bring healing to. Allow it to be there. Keep concentrating on whatever it is your issue is, and whilst you are letting it be there, keep breathing in and out, in and out. Say to yourself and to the issue, 'It's OK that you're there, it's OK that you're there'. Spend a few minutes doing this until you are ready to move onto the next step.

- Imagine a cross within a circle, and that you are travelling to the centre of the cross where the two lines intersect. You don't need to be able to visualise this, just have the intent that 'it is so'. Alternatively you can also have the intent that you are travelling inwards, going to the deepest place inside yourself, right into the centre of the centre. When you reach this place, imagine that you are 'grounding yourself in' (I see this as how a cat settles themselves in when they are sitting down to rest), and making a cosy spot for yourself to be there for a little while. Try not to over think any of these steps, just do it!

- Now that we are here (& don't worry about whether you are or not, as you keep practicing, it will become much easier very quickly and you will soon feel confident that you are here) and you are imagining yourself at the centre of the cross/ in the deepest part of your being, ask this part of yourself/ place in yourself to tell you anything you need to know about your issue. You could just ask 'What do I need to know right now?'. Then let yourself go quiet inside as you wait for an answer. Go with whatever first pops up into your head. Often, there will be an accompanying feeling, energy, image or colour with it.

- Then ask for healing for your issue. Again, let yourself go quiet and wait. Accept whatever comes, a feeling, a colour, an image or symbol. Magnify this, make it brighter or stronger, or larger, or whatever feels right. You can do any of the following; spread it out into your whole issue/situation, breathe it into your body, all your energy bodies, imagine your original issue, and see this healing moving through it (breathe it in, move it with your thoughts, etc), if it feels like an ancestral issue, send it into your ancestral line/ you can see this as a circle, those behind you are your past ancestors, those in front are your future ancestors, and yet you all meet up!! If it feels like a past life issue, send the healing into your past life/ lives and into all the moments in your current life where it has affected you. Take a few minutes to let the energy settle into you. Your energy system is readjusting itself now to the new energies.

- Ask yourself what the healing gift is in this for you. Simply create a quiet space inside yourself and stay open until it comes to you.

- Ask this part of you at the centre of yourSelf whether there is anything else that you need to know right now for your highest good, or anything else that needs healing.
- When you've finished, take some time to record your impressions and experiences, and do something quiet and gentle. Have something to drink or eat, or go for a walk to ground yourself and allow you to return yourself back to daily life.

You can do this practice every day

Once you have become used to going 'in' to the centre of yourself in this way, it can be a useful practice to use this technique whenever you want to create something, or you want to find out what it is that you want or would like to do. When we go inwards in this way, we are consulting our grounded higher self (which you could call your soul) that knows exactly what it wants to do here on the earth plane. In this way, we are drawing our wisdom from the purest part of ourselves. It is a very simple technique, and often this part of ourself will give us very simple advice; yet if we take a moment to reflect on the advice (or if you journal it, when you look back on it sometime later) we will often see that there is a depth and a wisdom to it that evidently belongs to our soul.

Many spiritual people are very good at meditating and going high into the light. And so for many of us, this simple practice of going inwards is a very useful technique that will help us balance & harmonise our heavenly and earthly selves.

'The Voice of your Soul' channeling

"Welcome all, I am Sarah.

The healing of yourself is the greatest task you can undertake in this lifetime. Until the healing is occurring within, mankind cannot heal itself on the outer layers of itself, ie, the society, culture and world that you live in. It is worthy of as much time and energy, focus and concentration as you can muster. Of course, what many of you already know is that as you do the inner work, the outer work seems to happen by itself. This means that as you heal your inner wounds, your lives take new paths & new directions and you are motivated to create those things in your lives that are for your highest good.

Think not that it is a selfish thing or an egotistical thing to devote all the moments that you can to your personal and spiritual growth; this is the moment in time that we are in, where we need to heal ourselves first; did not the master Jesus say 'physician, heal yourself'? And we are all physicians, inside us all is a little voice that we can learn to listen to, that tells us where to go for healing, what it is good for us, what we should avoid.

This is the voice of your intuition, and you would do well to practice and learn how to listen to it, because it is always leading you onto a path of healing & of wholeness, which is the way home, back to God/ Goddess. All of you have this voice, in the same way that all of you have a soul. Your intuition is the voice of your soul.

As in all things on the physical plane, everything has its counterpart. And it can be seen that you have a soul and a higher self. There are, of course, one and the same, but seen from different perspectives. Your soul is the heavenly part of yourself when seen from your inner-ness. Your Higher Self is the same part of you but one seen from your 'outer-ness'!

One is the immanent view. One is the transcendent view. And of course, you are one and the same. You are an immanent being and a transcendent being both at the same time, and not one or the other."

4 FINDING THE HEALING WITHOUT OF YOURSELF (CALLING ON THE TRANSCENDENT DIVINE)

Sometimes we need to look outside of ourselves for the healing that we need & Sarah's flame can connect us to the healing light of God. Sarah's flame is good for issues that feel a long way from ourselves, or that we feel lost with, or we don't know how to handle.

It is a way of finding the Divinity we need 'without' of ourselves. If you have an issue that you feel you need to hand over to someone else, or a higher power, call on Sarah's flame. It often brings a sense of oneness (unity consciousness), which can be invoked for group situations where there is conflict. The flame's energy is gentle and loving, patient and kind. It has been 'given' to me (in the sense of an intuitive knowing) that it can be used it a great deal for physical healing. You might need to do this a number of times before you get a result, for example, if you have an issue you need help with, you could do this every night for a week, or a month, or for as long as you felt was needed.

Sarah's Flame

(You can see a colour version of the flame at https://www.rachelgoodwin.dk/ascended-master-sarah)

Spend some time now sitting and looking at the picture of Sarah's flame, this will build a connection between you and the energy of the flame. If you can, print it out and have it around somewhere where you can see it often.

Ways of using the flame

- See your issue/ situation/ person surrounded by & infused by Sarah's flame.
- Breathe the energy of Sarah's flame into specific parts of your body where you are suffering disease.
- Ask Sarah to bring her flame to wherever it is you need the help.
- Imagine yourself sitting within Sarah's flame so that it envelops you.

Use the flame to write a healing intent & see the positive gifts within difficulties

Have your issue written down which could be, 'I never have enough money'. Imagine this infused with Sarah's flame. Then imagine what would be the polar opposite of this difficulty, 'I always have enough money, all my needs are met'. This then is the healing gift for you in this situation and is the spiritual truth for you to realise for yourself. Affirmations (as written about in many books that embraced the New Thought movement & widely popularised by Louise Hay) are a simple way to help these spiritual truths be manifested in your life. Spend a few minutes each day writing down your healing gift as an affirmation. (You can find a wealth of information on the internet and in self-help books if you need to learn how to write good affirmations)

'The Threefold Flame' channeling

Here is a transcript of a channelling about the flame:

Q- "What's the point Sarah of these 'flames'?!"

"Welcome all I am Sarah!

It is good to ask these things, and not just accept 'this is so', it is good to know WHY you should do a thing, instead of accepting blindly that this is the way forward, because it has been said that it is!

When God created the world, the Elohim imagined what was, and so it was! Humanity was their finest creation, and their greatest joy! Humanity has been made to reflect the Elohim; each person in humanity is playing an individual role, & no two are the same, and yet when we are all added up us a whole, we are the perfect whole; each one of us needed to make that whole.

And so it was with the Elohim, when creation was in the process of being formed, each one of them, in the circle of perfect love and light, did their own particular role, played their own particular part, no-one could do as the other did, only that one could do its own unique and needed part.

And so they loved and appreciated each other, as together they formed the miracle of creation!

And so has man been made in their likeness, each one of us perfect in our individuality, each one of us, within us, has only those God qualities and function which the Divine Presence (within us) has manifested, and each of us has our particular parts to play, that no other can do!

*But because we are living within linear time and space, (and I say we, because even though I am not here in an individual physical form, I am with you still in physicality (*authors note, Sarah has told me many times that she is in the etheric, and shines her light through each of us in the physical plane who connects with her*), then the Divine creation of humanity that the Elohim formed is still unfolding.*

It is not that the Elohim made creation and humanity to be an ever fixed form, and although at the moment of creation, all the elements of what it was, and will be in creation were ever present in the Original Blueprint of Perfection.
But creation is an ever-unfolding thing. You could see creation as aligned to the growing of a flower. First the seed starts to sprout because the right conditions for growth have been achieved, then the shoot starts to grow upwards in the darkness, emerging into the light. As the stem grows the bud of the flower grows larger and larger until the day where it starts to open and reveal the beauty hidden inside.

You could say (although this is not an exact analogy) that the Divine Masculine (the Christ Flame) is what is needed for the stem to grow tall and strong, straight and true, and then the Divine Feminine (the Magdalene Flame) is what is needed to form the perfect bud with all the beauty therein, and then you could say that the joining of these two perfect energies, into the union of the 3rd energy, the threefold flame which is what you know as Sarah's flame, is what causes the bud to reveal itself in all its true beauty.

And you could say that the saturation of the plant in each stage of its growth by exactly the right energy at exactly the right time is what causes everything to grow in the right way. That if the second energy came too soon, the bud would grow too big for the stem to support, and if the third energy came too late, then the stem would wither and die, before the flower had a chance to unfurl.

So although, as the Elohim had created, all of the elements were present in the original creation, the plan needed time to grow and unfurl with each element being present in right time, right place, and this is how the flames have assisted humanity in growing perfectly!

Right time, right place, right being! All is well!!

So it is not that the flames exist because you have something missing, or that you are deficient in some way, but that this is God's perfect plan for you built upon a rock, each element coming through of the plan in the perfect way to achieve the most beautiful and divine manifestation of heaven here on earth!

And so it is that my father and mother in heaven have prepared the way for me, and I am here now to facilitate the unfurling of the bud that holds all the beauty therein! This is my work and my power and is my perfect part to play in creation!

All is love, all is joy, all is perfect in wondrous creation… You can see as God sees…..Blessings, Sarah."

You can find a meditation for using the flame for healing at http://youtu.be/uDoQzM7bLxY

There's also an intro to the energy of the flame at http://youtu.be/5IabrY0qV4g

"Connecting to the light within has been a challenge for humankind, but now this is changing and becoming easier. Through my flame, you can be assisted to connect to your own Divine spark.

I am a bridge to the Christ consciousness & can help you feel & be your own divinity. Mankind is alchemizing his own lower, denser energies; making use of the unmolded clay and making it into something finer. Through the weaving of the light and the dark, (so the light becomes heavier and the dark becomes lighter) so that both are able to come into oneness, a 'being in the same place' & existing in the same time & space occurs, and a completion and wholeness are gained. The light knows the dark, and the dark knows the light, and in that knowing they are no longer separate but at one.

My flame allows/ assists in allowing everything to be as it is. It allows the dark to be there exactly as it is. It allows the light to be there exactly as it is. There is no resistance against what is. And in that allowing, the 'being' with things exactly as they are, transversely an alchemization takes place and something else occurs. Matter and spirit unite and become one. In this allowing, so does your state of being shift into unity consciousness. You are no longer keeping things separate or split off by judging what should be, or condemning things as wrong, or raising things one over the other by saying they are right & better. All is as it is. All is well."

5 AS WITHIN SO WITHOUT

The transcendent Divinity without of us and the immanent Divinity within us can be seen as one more example of the polarity in which we live. In her groundbreaking book, 'The goddess in the gospels', Margaret Starbird says,

"Whereas God the Father/Creator is honoured as the transcendent principle..the Holy Spirit is the immanent 'feminine' aspect of the Divine, ever guiding us from within".

Yet from another spiritual tradition, a sacred text written in the 13th century, Narayani (also known as Lakshmi) the goddess of manifest creation tells us about Narayana who exists outside manifest creation as the transcendent principle,

"There is no place where He exists without me. There is no place that contains me without containing Him...There is not a single place nor moment when it is possible for me to exist without Him, or for Him to exist without me."

That the transcendent and the immanent are separate from each other is an illusion.

Sarah holds the flame that connects us to our Divinity

Sarah holds in her hand the flame that connects us to our

divinity, and we can discover this within ourselves or without of ourselves, and although we experience them differently, they are one and the same. The simple but powerful & profound processes in this book are about accessing this divinity. If we choose to work with these processes deeply, we can raise our consciousness to a high enough vibration that these truths become clear to us. They are already true within us, because we already hold the divine oneness within us; it is what we are. Yet this understanding and knowledge remains hidden deep within our subconscious minds. With the support and guidance of Sarah's presence, we can 'make it so', and bring it into the light of our conscious awareness.

When we use these processes, the soul is often experienced as something very deep within us, and the Higher Self as a being of light that exists very far up in the higher dimensions, and yet they too are one and the same, just seen from a different perspective.

'The View from the Soul' channeling.

"The difference between the Higher Self and the Soul is simply one of perspective. When you look within yourself, you find the Soul, which seems to have more of an earthly grounded feel, an earthly wisdom; it understands the little things of your life.

When expanding your awareness out into the Higher realms, you find the Higher Self, a Divine being of great light, that seems to have little connexion or similarity to your little earthly being. And yet they are one and the same, they occupy the same space dimensionally. It is just how they look when viewed from different places; remember that when you receive wisdom and healing from the soul. Often it is very simple! Often the healing is very profound and yet seems to take no effort at all.

48

Because of this, it can be very easy to discount its value and holiness, even as what you receive from your inner wisdom causes profound changes in your life and consciousness.

So remember that your soul's light is the result of that great being of light (your higher self) being 'alive' on the earth plane. You have given your higher self an earthly home to embody through your physical life on this earth. You ARE your higher self on the earth, whether you remember it or not. IT IS SO!!

However, the more you can remember this, the more your consciousness is raised, and you can become more aware of it in wonderful, wonderful ways. When you connect to your inner wisdom and healing, this IS your Higher Self manifesting itself upon the earth, through the person that you are. You can learn to honour this as your inner Divinity speaking directly to you, & appreciate it as such'

What I see from this is that our higher self is what is seen on all layers and dimensional planes, but is seen differently depending on the dimensional plane from which it is viewed from. It's just that on the physical level, our H.S looks like a body, on the causal level it takes the appearance of the soul, on the auric plane it looks like the emotional body, but it is in actuality always the higher self and nothing else! We don't see this, because our awareness isn't there yet, not because it isn't so.

In Sarah's presence all things come into Oneness

In her presence, all things come into oneness, dark and light, heaven and earth, male and female. We move from a place of polarity in our consciousness into one of unity. We start to have the realisation that polarity is an illusion from a spiritual perspective. A polarity cannot exist individually, it has to have its counterpart. Dion Fortune

(1993) explains the meaning of this beautifully,

"..each taken separately, is a great half-truth, and so misleading. They must therefore never be considered apart. This is course, is true of any symbol, which must always be considered in relationship to its opposite if a full understanding is to be obtained of its significance, for all manifestation is dual, Unity being Unmanifest."

Outside of manifest creation the divine is in its original transcendent state of oneness. This is the energy that Sarah's flame invokes, and we respond to it, because inside each of us is our original spark of creation. In Vedic teachings (Farrand 2006) Narayana dreams as he floats in a sea of inky blackness & as he does this creation is formed; as each being is created, he places inside each one a piece of his own divine substance (our divine spark). This spark is called the **Hrit Padma** or sacred heart,

"It is located between the fourth and fifth chakras, three finger-widths below the heart in the front of the chest, & is considered in Vedic teachings to be the seat of the soul" Thomas Ashley-Farrand.

Thus we meet again the paradox, as above, so below, as within, so without. The transcendence is within us and without of us.

Be your own unique & beautiful Essence

Sarah shows us our path to healing so we can be our own beautiful essence. We already know we want to heal, because we want to feel better than we do, or because we don't want to suffer, or because we want the world to be a better place.

Sarah wants to help us find the essence of who we are, to find our uniqueness.

"Each of us holds the key to manifesting God's plan here on earth. Each of us holds deep in our heart, the seeds to our own joy & happiness. Each of us needs to dig deep now, & prepare the ground for the planting of the New Age. What colour shall your garden be, what size, what shape? You get to choose; it is your desire that will show you the way forward, what plants you need to pick. Each of you holds your own individual piece of the puzzle, without which the picture will be incomplete. You see how important you are, how special, how divine? What will you choose?" Sarah.

Your mission on Earth

Sarah teaches us to dig down deep inside ourselves and find the essence of who we are. Her presence lends us the vision to see our own truth and what we truly want in our lives. Her message is very simple, 'be who you are'. God's perfect plan is built upon a rock; it is ever changing, always adapting itself as we live our lives and make the choices of free will. The Divine is always bringing into incarnation those of us who are ready for the job at hand and have the necessary skills and soul qualifications to get the job done. Only the Divine can see the whole picture, but each of us is given everything we need to know through the divine sense of our intuition. That is why at this time so many of us are developing our psychic and spiritual gifts; in this way we can sense, hear or see God's divine plan and gain the guidance that we need.

'The Centre of yourSelf' channeling

"Welcome all. I am the ascended lady master Sarah.

Today I have come to speak to you of the physical shells of which you inhabit and their entry way into the world. Many of the world's most spiritual religions have been dedicated to teaching how to cast off the body so as to liberate the spirit 'trapped' inside, to allow the soul to reside within 'nirvana', the higher spiritual dimensions.

Today I wish to speak to you of how the higher self can inhabit your physical body and become more nearly the way in which through you can be in contact with nirvana, in fact of all of creation, all of the time. These are the mysteries I have come to teach.

Your body is your physical tool here on this earth; it is how you will affect change here on the physical planes. The ascended masters, the angels and archangels, all can assist and help from the realms within which we exist; we can gently persuade and create optimum conditions from within which the best possible chances for change and transformation can occur. But it is YOU that has the power to create the New Earth here in physical manifestation, and in so many more ways than you know.

At the point where heaven meets earth in your bodies, between the heart and solar plexus, so am I. I have come to reawaken that which lies dormant within yourselves, already my light, my love dances secretly across the earth, skipping and laughing that the miracles of life which are yourselves are beginning the long thaw to your spiritual spring.

And in my secret dance, I would whisper stories of hidden

chakras, lying nestling under the snow, simply waiting for all to melt, so it can reveal its magnificence. Humanity........creation is your birthright, and within you, you have the power to create, not just your own lives, but universes as well.

At the point where heaven meets earth in your bodies, so I am. Here is the entry point to your souls, your higher Selves. Not high above you in some far away dimension, but here, right at the Centre of yourselves. Here is all things, and no-thing, manifest and unmanifest creation. From here will New Humanity start to live, here at the Centre of themSelves, at the Centre of all things.

To assist you in your lives, you can call on me, my light, my love, by bringing your attention to me, to the balance point in between your heart centre and your solar plexus. Breathe into this space, feel your awareness. BE here. Breathe into this space whenever 'mind' has taken over, and you need to re-connect with yourSelves.

Chant and call on me,

OM SRI SARAYEI NARAYANI NAMOSTUTE (Om Shree Sah-ra-yei Na-rah-yan-nee Na-moh-stoo-the)

Om and salutations to Sara, the three fold flame, bestow upon us the highest blessings

Say to yourself, as you breathe into yourSelf, 'I am here, I am at the centre of myself, I am in the moment, in the Now, at the centre of all things, I am here.'

You are upon your mission to become more of who you are, a nara-narayani, your higher self here in full manifestation upon the earth.

The most powerful truths are often the most simple, and yet can be the most complicated to explain, for now let it suffice to say, that if you wish to live more from your divine self, using the precious resource of your physical body, then this simple breathing exercise can help you achieve this goal, throughout your daily life.

Blessings be upon you all, beauteous web of light spread across the earth. Blessed are you that these secrets are being revealed to you now, use them well, embrace them into your own lives, contemplate upon the profound truths which are being given to you now. Do not search for cleverness and complicated sophistications; these are not truths to be understood by your minds, but wisdoms which can only be felt in the truth of your hearts.

Allow yourselves to practice being at the centre of yourSelves, and watch the magickal mysteries of your lives unfold before you.

And remember, there at the centre of yourSelves, there you will find me. Blessings, Blessings, Blessings, Namaste my beautiful ones, Namaste. All is well. Sarah."

6 CHANNELINGS FOR HEALING

Blessings for the Heart

'Welcome all, I am Sarah.

Today I would speak to you of the Divine, of the union that is between you. (and in reality there is no 'union', you are simply one!)

In all things God is there.

In the difficult things in your life, God is there.

In the wonderful things in your life, God is there.

In all things God is there, in you, with you, around you.

You are never separate.

But the part of you, that reasons and rationalises, and when things are difficult thinks consciously or unconsciously in a way that creates thoughts such as, 'this has happened because I am unworthy, unloved, unliked', or 'I have failed again, why am I so unworthy?'; this part of you has become separated from God, this part of you is not resonating with your God consciousness, and is thinking incorrect thoughts, creating despair, depression, anger, rage, bitterness, resentment, sadness, apathy and so on.

How to hold this part of yourSelf up to the light then?

How to keep this consciousness within your inner Divinity?

If you notice then, that there is a part of you that, for example, believes the world is a terrible place, that bad things happen out there to good people, and maybe it would be better not to be here on the earth in such a painful place, you could take this part of you and bless it with the light. Imagine some difficulty now that is your own.

You could imagine that I am sitting in front of you, that we are sitting there together, facing each other, and you could imagine that you hold out this part of you, this difficulty in yourself and that you hold it there cupped in your hands.

You could imagine that my hands are held out too, that you rest your hands cupped there on top of mine.

As you imagine it there in our hands, you could think of the times that this part of you has come out in your life, and think of what it has created for you. You could remember how it feels when you are living from this part of yourself.

Feel, imagine and remember the very worst bits of how this issue plays out for you, and put it all there in the palms of your hands. You could simply think of the energy of this part of yourself, as maybe you know it very well, and hold that there, cupped in the palms of our hands. Instruct yourself to place anything else that needs to be there, and allow the last pieces to flow into your open hands.

And then simultaneously at the same time, from both of our hearts, you can see two arcs of light, one from mine, and one from your own going down into the palms of your hands, blessing this part of you with the light.

See, feel or imagine the light filling all of the things you have placed there in the palms of our hands.

And you can hold this issue there until it is completely bathed in light, and until it has absorbed all that it needs. You don't have to see this part of you being healed or changed, you don't need to 'do' anything to it, just allow it to soak up what it needs from the light we are both sending from our hearts.

See, feel or just simply know that our hands are filled now with the most incredible light, that it seems incredible that our hands can hold this much light and then gently, with love and gratitude, bring all of this back to your heart; the light and your difficulty and place it back in your heart.

You could place your hands over your heart if you

wished while you do this.

If your heart feels closed, call on me and ask me to open it for you; give yourself time with the meditation, allow it to unfold slowly, slowly, and then when you see, feel or become aware of the first chinks of light in your heart as it becomes open, the beautiful light you are holding in your hands rushes in through the smallest aperture, the smallest opening to your heart. Or maybe for you the light flows into the most incredibly open space that is your heart centre.

However it happens for you, all is well. It is as it is. All is well.

Breathe that beautiful light back into your heart centre, held together now with all of your pain and difficulties; welcome it all home.

All is God.

Expect miracles as your pain and difficulties are being healed now by the light and love you have showered upon it reveal their hidden truths to you.

Perhaps telling you what they were and why they were there, or what it is they have become; for each of you a unique truth, just exactly what you needed to know on your life path right now.

Take some time to find out what it wants you to know, take some pen and paper, write it down, discover the incredible light within yourself, and the wisdom that you carry.

I am Sarah.

Blessings are upon us, each and every day of our lives.

All is well, all is well, all is well.'

No Train To Miss

'I am love. I am light. I am life.

I am in all things.

You are finding your way through the pain that is between you and God.

It is the distance between you.

To go into that pain is a painful and difficult process.

My blessings can be the light in the darkness, if that is where you are, or they can be the spark that will plunge you into the darkness, if you have immersed yourself only in the light.

Wherever it is that you have not been, that is where my blessings will take you.

Into the unexplored, the unintegrated, that which has been kept separate from yourself.

All of which, of course, happens with the consent of your higher self, your own inner divine authority.

My spark, my blessing, adds an extra hand, and extra step up along the way – isn't it always so?

Because you are already on the way, being the divine beings that you are.

My blessings are an extra intermediary measure, bringing an extra quality of evolution, of bringing something new and unexplored into the equation; but always with the consent of your higher self, who you could say has put me in the path of you, so that you can take my qualities on now, at this moment in your life where I can be the most useful.

All the things that you need in your life, God (you) is always bringing to you.

All the things that you need in your life, you (God) is always going towards.

Your journey's destination is assured. Your journey back home to yourSelf.

It can help to remember this!!!

There is only one final destination for you; unity consciousness/ oneness/ wholeness/ integration.

Knowing this, perhaps you can take a little more note of where you are right now & just breathe it in. Breathe it in.

You can be here. It's OK.

There's no rush. No train to miss.

You are always coming back home.

Back to yourSelves.

Back to the Divine.

You are there already, it is just your consciousness that

is learning how to place itself there too.

All is well little ones, all is well, let yourself grow, let yourself be the seedlings that you are right now, struggling up towards the light, delicate, tender… all is well.

Blessings be upon you, Sarah.'

Breathe Life Into…

'Here we are again with the light and the dark.

How to bring the light into the dark.

All those spaces in your life where difficulty and darkness exist.

What has come with you ancestrally, your inheritance.

The unmoulded clay.

This is life which is waiting for God to be brought into it, waiting for the light to be breathed into it. It is your work, why you are here.

For you to find out how you can breathe the light of God into your life.

Into all that doesn't bring you joy, or happiness or peace.

These are the things for you to breathe the light of life into.

Not to change, or eradicate, rise above or destroy, but simply to bring God to.

The missing ingredient!

The difficulties, the challenges, the frustrations; they are all your indicators saying, 'yes, work with this',and, 'notice me, notice me, I am your work' .

They are not here to punish you and make you suffer, but

it is for you to take notice and carry out your life's purpose, bringing the light of God, the light of yourSelves to bear on these things.'

As Without So Within

'Welcome all, I am Sarah.

Today, I have come to speak to you of the power to change, and the joy that this brings.

When you look around you, and you see the world in disarray, do not worry, do not have fear, it is merely showing you where you need to heal.

It is showing you, where you need to heal, not outside of you, but inside of you.

Now surely, you may think, I can't be responsible for the problems of the world?!

Well, what is the world?

Is the world not your internalised consciousness projected and externalised outside of you?!

Now this is not to say that you now have the task of singlehandedly clearing up the whole world around you, but that what is without is within, and what is within, you have the power of dominion over!

So listen again, when you look around you, and you see the world in disarray, (or your boss, or your car, job etc), do not fear, it is merely showing you where you need to heal.

This is a message of hope, because all that is within you can be given to God, (or the Divine, or the Goddess, or the Angels and so on, whatever you resonate with).

The Divine has the power to heal all, to take all that is not of the Divine, and clear and cleanse and to make whole again.

This power to change, is the power of the Divine to make anything 'good' again. We don't even have to know why, or how that 'wrongness' is there, although sometimes for the purpose of our conscious ego's it can help to facilitate the change.

But what we do need to do is call upon the power of the Divine, (which is also our Divine Selves, for we are the Divine, and the Divine is us) to transmute and transform whatever it is that is within us that needs healing……….

"Dear Divine Father/Mother, I am seeing in the world, (for example, I am seeing in my friend/partner/boss, for example, illness, negativity, addiction), and it is troubling me. I ask of your Divine Grace, your gentle love, that all that is within me that resonates with this is healed and cleansed, cleared and transformed, and I ask this for my highest good and the benefit of all beings. Please forgive me for my own issues, that have contributed to this, and help me to be aware of what my issues are and I thank you Divine Mother/Father for your Divine Grace in clearing away this from within me.

Blessings be upon you, I love you, Blessed Be, Blessed Be, Blessed Be.'

Forgive Each Other

'Welcome all, I am Sarah.

There is at this time on the earth, a need for forgiveness for the last age, the Piscean Age.

In this time, there have been many transgressions against the Divine Feminine, just as in the age before that, (an age lost out of time and memory), where the Divine Feminine held sway, there were many transgressions against the Divine Masculine.

Many of you remember this time for it's goodness in the honouring of the Divine Mother, and so it was, that there were many good things, but there was darkness too.

Many wounds are coming to the surface in each of you individually, in healing the dark times you have been through, where your gifts of seerhood and magick which are associated with the Divine Feminine were systematically torn from you, through a legacy of torture and abuse, repeated over and over again down through the ages, until they came to be no more, or very little in the cultures within which you live.

Now the Divine Feminine is re-appearing from her long absence, rising up from the depths, and making herSelf known once again, and once again she is living in you, through you, for you.

But it is not enough for you to demand recompense and justice for the wrongs which have been done to you.

To acknowledge the wounds and injustices, yes, this is needed and very much the right thing. It is truth that in this last age, these things have happened, that terrible wounds have been created, and that it was the actions of the masculine against the feminine.

Now that you can see more clearly what the wounds are, what the damage has been, so that you can start to heal and tend to what needs your loving care, now is also coming the time for you to let go of your anger over the injustices that has occurred.

If you think of a child that has been doing terrible things, that has gone astray and become monstrous in its actions – imagine now, 'what will help this child heal?'

Would it help for this child to receive tender loving care and to be given an opportunity to see what it has done, so that a new way can be found?

Or would it help to be shouted at, and told what a terrible person it is, that it deserves to suffer for what it has done?

Deep within the unconsciousness of the feminine is this anger and urge to beat the masculine into submission, until the masculine lies weeping on the floor, saying sorry for it's terrible transgressions, and then the feminine may take up her rightful place once again, take back her power and rise above the masculine, so that all may be kept in its rightful place.

This side of the feminine has been denied, as we stick to the cultural myths that women are all loving mothers, wives and friends that exude the love of the Divine Mother over all, and forget the heritage which we have inherited and the terrible truth of the power of the Dark Mother, and her ability to wield suffering in hidden ways!

At this moment in time, all of us have the opportunity to forgive the Divine Masculine, whether we are male or female.

All of us have lived through the Piscean Age in forms of male and female, and so in truth we are forgiving ourselves for our ability to make someone 'the other' and then punish it for its perceived wrongdoing!

This is the truth, that in transgressing against others we transgress against ourselves.

That in holding forgiveness from others, we keep forgiveness from ourself and keep ourself in a state of separation consciousness instead of unity consciousness.

There is no other, only ourselves, which is all one and all God!

If you made a mistake, would you want to be forgiven for it, and given the opportunity to find out why you made that mistake and what you can learn from it?

Or would you want to be blamed, and told what an evil monster you were?!!

Every time we blame someone, we make them other from ourSelves, we are denying that we are all one and part of the same Divine consciousness.

When we refuse love in our hearts for others, and refuse to make a bid for understanding, then this is what we are doing to ourselves, and so the cycle of hurt and blame and accusation continues.

What can be done then?

Firstly, we can set an intent for forgiveness,

'And be ye kind one to another, tenderhearted, forgiving one another, even as God for Christ's sake hath forgiven you' (Ephesians 4:32)

In that intent, we can remember that we are all one, aspects of the Godhead and that if someone is transgressing against us with what seems like deliberate intent, then they are unable to remember this divine truth.

'Father forgive them, for they know not what they do' shows the Christ Jesus's intent for forgiveness, even as he was being physically tortured, dying and in terrible pain on the cross.

This then we can emulate, though our brother and sister gives us pain in what they do, we can still seek forgiveness for them in our hearts, and keep looking for it there.

This practice can with discipline be continued until we find forgiveness there, because it is there, because we are God, and all that is within God is within us.

71

God forgives us for every second of every day, the flow of forgiveness is neverending and absolute. In this forgiveness so can we flourish and prosper and become our true Selves, knowing ourSelves as Christ.

In this age can we learn to manifest the flow of forgiveness for each other, so we can help each other to live in the flow of forgiveness and manifest the beauty of our Divinity here on the earth.'

7 CHANNELINGS FOR LOVE

Loving Yourself As God
From Anna, Great Grandmother of Sarah

'Now is the time for you to learn to love yourself as God loves you!

Do you think that God looks down upon you each day, and feels disappointment?!

No, this disappointment comes from inside yourself, that you haven't been as you've wanted to be – but this is your egoic self talking, not God!

You're looking at other people and thinking that because you're not successful as they are successful, that you have failed.

Have you ever thought that perhaps God has a different plan for you?

That if you were being successful like them, in fact you would have failed?!!!

Because this is not God's plan for you.

(God's perfect plan is built upon a rock)

I know that this is a hard lesson to learn, to love yourself as God loves you, but much of the pain is caused by holding onto the pain of not being as others have wanted you to be, or of trying to be as you imagine others have wanted you to be.

And still finding that you fall short of the mark!

All these little pains from this life and others, add up to one big pain that holds all the rejection, the loss, the disappointments, the judgements, the feeling less than & not enough.

And when you stand back and see the whole sorry mess for what it is, you have to,

a) acknowledge the pain that you feel (& give up trying to protect yourself from it) and b) realise how much of this you have unwittingly taken on from the outside world, and then carried it around with you as if it were the God's honest truth itself!

So do that now – summon your courage and have a good long look at this pain that you carry.

What does it look like?

Notice where it's located, in your body, or somewhere around you.

Notice whether it has a colour, or size or shape, or even a name or temperature.

How does it feel?

And then ask it, why are you here?

What purpose do you have?

And see or hear or feel what it says to you.

So do this now, take a few moments to quietly imagine these things, and then notice what the difference is.

Was there any purpose to this pain, other than to hide the truth of you?

Say to yourself, 'I love myself and who I am, I love myself and who I am, I love myself and who I am.

I am, I am, I am.'

And repeat as much as you want! Say these words over

to yourself until you feel a grounding basis of truth within it.

And lay upon yourself the Sacred Task of loving yourself & who you are.

Say to yourself, 'Never again will I allow others to create this illusion around me!'

'It is my Sacred Task to love myself & who I am.

I lay this Sacred Task upon me!'

And make this commitment to yourself that never again will you lay upon yourself the need to meet other's expectations & try to make them happy in this way.

Be true to yourself, to what you want, to how you feel.

Do it with love & compassion, but always honour WHO YOU ARE & WHAT YOU NEED!

This is God's wish for you, & mine.

May blessings be upon you, each & every day of your life.

Anna.

Upon The Subject Of Love

There is much to be said upon the subject of love!

As with many simple things, their very simplicity requires deep and profound comprehension to be understood by the human intellect, and so many books could be written upon the subject of love.

This simplicity requires a purity of understanding, one that is not weighted down by worldly concerns, and worries of the ego.

If you are seeing through the eyes of the ego then that is how you will understand love, in terms that the ego understands.

If you are seeing through the eyes of God, then that is how you will understand love, as God understands love, and you can do this by connecting to the God within you, the divine presence which is inside of you.

Through the eyes of the ego, love will always be a thing to be won and lost. Something in black and white, which is either there or not there.

Something to be given or something to be gained.

So it is only through contacting the Divine within yourself that you can truly appreciate how God loves you, how you are loved.

As a manifestation of God in the physical world, you have given God something to love outside of itself.

It can see you, as it were in front of itself, and it can love you for everything that you are.

God is able to see all of you, your hopes and fears, your loves and doubts, your worries and concerns.

God is able to see all of this and more, and still see your shining glory, your beauty, your divinity. She sees where this has taken you and what you are able to do with it.'

To Connect You To Love

'Welcome all, I am Sarah.

Today I would talk to you again on the nature of Divine Love, how this is a quality which you can learn to give to yourselves, from yourSelves!

As we have talked about before, there are many situations in your world, that if you had been able to invite in the energy of Divine Love, would have been greatly eased.

For example, if you think about the terrible pain between the nations of Israel and Palestine, the wounds that have been caused. Justice will not heal this rift, nor patience, nor strength. Only Love.

And so it is in your own lives, the worst pain that you find there, the most terrible things that have happened, can only be healed by the power of Divine Love.

At these times, when pain is all around and you don't know what to do, or how to respond, turn inwardly into yourselves and ask yourSelf what Love would do?

It might be that you need to remove yourself from the situation, or tell someone that because of the love you have for yourself, you cannot allow yourself to be in such a situation any longer.

It might be that you need to go away and make yourself a bowl of soup!

But if we respond to the trauma and conflict in our lives, in this way, with love for ourselves, we are always acting from Love, instead of rage and pain, and this Love can be more real inside ourselves than what is happening 'out there', and you can infect a whole situation with the Divine energy of Love!

If you ask yourself, 'what can I do for myself in Love?', then you are not shouting or adding to the trauma. It may be that it comes to you, to explain how you feel.

But doing it from Love, you can be calm and careful of yourself, because you are looking after yourself, and meeting your own needs to be loved and no longer in trauma, pain or shock.

And the Loving thing to do in each situation will be totally different, and Love will always give you the answer that you need.

And only You can give these things to yourself and no other!

In finding these things inside yourSelf, this Divine Love, you are bringing God onto the earth and into your everyday reality and existence, and all is well, all is well, all is well!

May blessings shine down upon you each and every day of your lives!

Blessed Be, Blessed Be, Blessed Be,

Sarah.'

8 THE CHRIST SARAH…

I Am The Presence Of Christ

'Welcome I am the Presence of Christ.

I am that which resides in your soul, waiting to be awakened from my sleep, waiting for the call to arms that indicates a soul's readiness to be reunited with their true nature.

For in truth, my energy is neither male nor female, though the Christ Jesus may be understood in this way in conjunction with the mystery of the Magdalene.

The truth of the energy of the Christ, is that this is the part of humanity that stayed behind in the loftier places when the rest of the matrix of humanity descended down further into matter.

I am your divinity made manifest on earth, but still my energy is redolent more of heaven than of earth, and so is a little 'distant' for many to connect.

In this age, where Christianity has brought so much history with it, Christianity bears many wounds and stigmas that belong to a past time, a past age.

And so it is fitting that now I pass my cross to Sarah. Sarah, the Christ Child, Sarah the Great One; Sarah who carried within her the seeds of the New Humanity and lived on earth, hidden, unknown, but all the same, there, real, and waiting for those to find her that are ready to hear the message of Christ lives on through us all.

As my presence was once embodied on the earth, through the Christ Jesus, I was able through the resurrection and the ascension of Christ Jesus, to leave the imprint there, of what had once been separated, now co-joined once again. The Ascended body of Christ Jesus, made manifest upon the earth, leaving the imprint, the blueprint, in the earth matrix, of heaven made manifest upon the earth, the divine blueprint, the original blueprint of perfection. Showing you what is to come, what will be, showing you your true potential as God intended you should be made manifest here on the earth.

A circuitous route has been taken granted, but yet, through the glory of heaven all will be well, and man will shine upon the earth, with his glorious body of ascension, his physical body as God intended it to be, humanity's original blueprint of perfection, made manifest here on earth.

And so you see, that you are the miracles, the human being, once again ascending to their destiny of being the beings they were meant to be, with their incorruptible body of light, and the denser matter laid behind, a phase in the evolution now of humanity's soul.

*But Sarah lived the life here. She received the blueprint
of the original blueprint of perfection for the physical
body direct from her father, held as she was, a child still,
within the auric energy of her parent, Christ Jesus. She
walked with it in her energy field, here on the earth, she
held the patterns static and safe in her energy body,
carried in the outer edges of her auric field, until the
time when humanity was ready to receive the key for
these mysteries, these potentials to be unlocked.*

*Sarah is the key, she is the way to ascension. She holds
the energy of Christ, but here, closer to the earth, and on
the etheric plane. The presence of Christ as it was
manifested through the Christ Jesus, was the first time it
had ever been on the earth, and had previously only
existed in heaven. Sarah carries that energy as it is since
it has been brought to earth, since it has been used to
alchemise the physical body, as her father did in his
great achievement of the resurrection, she took this on,
this great achievement, and carried it for her lifetime
which she lived in France and other places, and so is the
energy of the resurrected body, which is all our
destinies, imprinted on the earth, in the earth matrix,
into the very rocks and stones where Sarah lived, and as
Sarah, and Christ too, were part of humanity, so is the
blueprint for the ascended physical body of perfection,
part of the matrix of humanity, and is there available to
us all.*

*Of course, I do not mean to say that each member of
humanity must know Sarah to become ascended, Divine
Truths are Divine Truths, and there are many different*

paths to opening up to our Divinity.

What I mean to say is that the Christ Jesus was the instrument of the Divine's will in manifesting the Christ Light here on earth, and each member of humanity has now the Christ potential within them, whether they 'believe in' Christ or not.

And in the same way, Sarah is the instrument of the Divine's will in taking humanity forward so that they may unlock this Christ potential within themselves, carrying on her father's legacy.

In this I do not mean to deny the Magdalene by omitting her name, more rather, that in this sense she is the hidden part of the Christ, for the Christ presence fully manifested through the Christ Jesus Magdalene, who are in truth one being and that this is held within the archetype of the Christ Sarah.

And so are you all Christed beings, Christ is within you all, and this is coming to pass for more and more of you that you are remembering, on an energetic level, you are awakening the Christ force within you, and so it is within the matrix of humanity that a beautiful light is arising, and slowly but surely this gentle glow is shining out to all those around.

As Christ is within you, so my presence, the presence of the Christ will softly manifest more and more around you, drifting down softly from the heavens, like gentle clouds and cloaks of the presence and light of Christ.

Sarah will continue to guide you, if you hear her call,

*calling you onwards, with courage, bravery and
determination, calling your earthly part to arms, to win
the most glorious prize of your GodSelves made manifest
here on earth.*

*Blessings upon you all, may your lights shine bright in
the darkness, and draw you all together to create a light
so bright that there may be none who no longer see.*

*I breathe my gentle breath of light upon your Christ
presences, so that you may receive strength and succour
to continue your paths of light.*

Blessed be.'

AFTERWORD

My journey with Sarah has been a long and intense one. Her continued and invited presence in my life has had a remarkable cathartic effect. Sarah has led me towards what is real, and away from what is unreal. She has continually lifted the veil of illusion and shown me the truth, about myself, about others, and all of the things in my life. In return, I have cleared, cleansed, opened my eyes and allowed myself to see, transformed, transmuted, taken upon myself spiritual practices through thick and thin, done my best to learn the spiritual lessons I've been shown and develop the spiritual qualities needed. I've had times of great difficulty and doubt, but she's never left me, even when maybe I wished she would!!

In Her, I have found mySelf.

This isn't an easy path to walk, but for those who want to 'turn their face to God', Sarah's path is a powerful one.

Sarah came to me after I had been channeling for a few years. She wasn't someone that I 'believed' in, and I have no particular attachment to various stories or myths about her. In fact I love them all!! Just as there are often many versions of fairy tales, so I think there is room for many different versions of stories about Sarah. Just as there is in fairy tales a deep & underlying philosophical truth, so I think it is with all the myths and legends surrounding Sarah and the holy family. There is no right or wrong here, only spiritual truth to be found and discovered by our souls. This is what Sarah means to me, spiritual truth and a way home to mySelf.

Connecting with Sarah doesn't need complicated rituals, (but of course, if you like them and enjoy them, then that is the thing for you to do!) nor does she need you to have advanced spiritual knowledge or techniques in order to bring her presence into your life.

She just needs you to ask.

HEALING SYSTEM WITH
SARAH & THE ANGELS

Want to go further and deeper with healing with Sarah?

You can receive initiations into Sarah & the Angels Healing System!

1st level – you are initiated into and attuned to Sarah's Angels white healing ray.

2nd level – you are initiated into and attuned to Sarah's violet flame

3rd level – you are initiated into and attuned to Sarah's green ray of healing

4th level – you are given all of the symbols for using with advanced healing methods

5th level – you are taught how to initiate others into Sarah and the Angels healing system.

Visit rachelgoodwin.dk to find out more or to contact Rachel for class dates.

APPENDIX

3 week suggested healing journey with Sarah

Week 1 Day one:
- call on the violet flame
- call on Sarah to help you (see chapter 1)
- tell her what it is you want to heal & why
- create a healing intent/ affirmation using the flame (chapter 4)

Rest of the week
- do violet flame exercise every day
- write/ speak or sing your healing intent/ affirmation every day for several minutes
- add any other practices of your own that you feel are relevant
- keep a journal for the 3 weeks using the process of Allowing*

Week 2
- create Sarah's healing circle each day & sit in Sarah's presence for 5/10 minutes each day
- ask questions or just sit in meditation
- continue to write/ speak or sing your healing intent/ affirmation every day for several minutes
- look back over your journal for the last 2 weeks and highlight the issues that jump out at you, &/or sit in meditation and reflection and see what

insights you gain on the issues.
- one by one take these into the healing circle with you and either do the inner resources journey or Sarah's healing flame journey

Week 3

- create a collage or drawing of your healing intent or your healing goal. You could find a symbol or a picture in a magazine that gives you the same feeling as your healing intent does. Put it up somewhere where you can see it regularly and every day
- every day write, sing or draw 'I love .... (the universe supporting me) all is well every day spend a few minutes imagining that your healing intent/ affirmation has come true. How does it feel?
- Play the 'as if' game. Imagine that your healing goal has come true. What things can happen now in your life? What's different about your daily life? Be completely spontaneous. Brainstorm. Imagine it with no limits, as if anything can happen, and miracles abound in your life. Play with it and have fun.
- Look back over your journal for the last three weeks, and take in the journey that you have been on, the changes that have occurred, and what has shifted within you.
- Give thanks to Sarah for all the blessings that you have received. Blessed Be and Amen!!

*Allowing. These are powerful energies that will usually bring things up for you. Make a practice of accepting what comes up for you. Journal whatever it is that comes up, and allow the words & feelings to flow out onto the page without censoring any of it. Let it be there. Being honest with yourself like this is your journey to wholeness (& not cutting away or repressing the bits you don't like or worry aren't acceptable). Practice doing this right from the start. The more you allow things to come up, the more light you can bring in.

Timing your Healing Journey

You can time your healing journey, if you wish with the moon phases to complement your healing process, and so utilise the power of the physical universe that you are living within. Solar eclipses & lunar eclipses are times of transformational change. So too are the equinoxes and solstices. You can also utilise the calendar of spiritual & religious events ie, over Christmas/ Easter there are some very special spiritual energies available to us.

Single Session Journey for Yourself

- light a candle to Sarah
- cast Sarah's healing circle around you
- call on Sarah to help you (see chapter 1)
- imagine Sarah is putting the violet flame around you
- tell her what it is you want to heal & why
- create a healing intent/ affirmation (write it down on a piece of paper or have an object/ drawing that symbolises it for you)
- put your healing intent in the centre of the circle
- do the inner or the outer journey
- journal your experiences (some people might actually like to write it down as they go, or speak it into a recording device.

If you are a healer or therapist, & when you feel comfortable & familiar with working with these processes, you can use them with other people in your healing practice.

Working with Dreams

- Light a candle to Sarah & if you have one, place a picture of Sarah near you.
- You can have a favourite crystal or stone to hold in one hand whilst you are doing this exercise.
- Cast Sarah's healing circle around you (a quick way to do this is just to draw the boundaries around you in your mind's eye; starting at the front of you, draw a line all the way around yourself in a circle and go round three times in all. Then extend it out above you, below you, to your left and to your right, so that you are sitting in a sphere.)
- Imagine Sarah's presence entering the circle. Feel yourself grounded in her Presence.
- See her surrounding you in her violet flame. This allows you to see what is real, and leads you away from what is unreal.
- Write down the dream that you had (or if you've already written it down, read it through.)
- Ask 'what do I need to know about this dream?' (ask 3 times, then go quiet)
- Write down/ speak what comes to you.
- Ask 'how can I heal this?' (or transform, or clear, or whatever is relevant)
- Ask 'is there anything else I need to know?'

Ancestral Healing Journey

Many of us have made soul agreements to help clear our ancestral lines, and often issues have been passed down to us through family generations. There might be particular things that you are already aware of that you would like to clear, or you can do a more general clearing.

To help with this you can try the following exercise.

- Call on Sarah and ask her to help you. Imagine her energy is all around you. Ask Sarah for any guidance that she wants to give you about this matter. If you don't have a specific issue to clear, ask Sarah what it is you should clear right now. (or feel inside yourself and ask yourself this question)
- Imagine that you are sitting inside a circle. It is a cross within a circle. Close your eyes & imagine that energetically now, you are journeying to the centre of that circle. When you get there, make yourself comfortable, and ground yourself in, nice & deep!
- From this place, you have access to all of your soul's wisdom & healing.
- Ask if there is anything you need to know right now about this issue. Doing this might put you in touch more deeply with what the issue is, or you might receive some information or something else.
- Focusing your awareness very clearly on where you are in the centre of that circle, ask for healing for this situation/ issue. Open yourself to receive & then sit and wait. Notice what comes up. Accept whatever comes first.
- Ask yourself (you can write this if you want),

'what does it feel like?', 'if it had a colour what would it be', 'what kind of energy is it?', 'what does that colour/ energy/ feeling mean/ represent to me?' Some of the questions will give you more information than others, that's fine. Go with what you get.

- Imagine it growing stronger. Feel it rushing through you as you focus on it more and more, bringing it into being. You are still at the centre of the circle. Imagine a circle of your ancestors around you who suffered from this difficulty/ issue, and send out to them the healing. Send it round to the left or the right or even both ways. These are your ancestors, past, present, future. You could see the healing energy you're sending building up and up, from the bottom to the top, until the whole circle is glowing.

- Now see your own timeline running through you, with the past, present & future. Send the healing along the timeline, forward and back, all around to all the times when you suffered from this difficulty/ issue. See a time where something happened to you recently that brought this issue up, and send it the healing as well.

- When/ if this issue gets triggered for you, bring in/ breathe in the healing colour/ energy/ feeling you received.

- If you'd like to, ask Sarah why this issue has been there in your family line, and why it was the right time to heal it now.

BIBLIOGRAPHY

Ashley-Farrand, Thomas. Healing Mantras. New York: Random House, 1999.

Fortune, Dion. The Magical Battle of Britain. Bradford on Avon, Wiltshire: Golden Gates Press, 1993.

Gupta, Sanjukta. Laksmi Tantra: a Pancaratra Text. Delhi: Motilal Banarsidass, 2003.

Jung, C. G., Vol XIV of the Collected Works, Mysterium Coniunctionis: An Inquiry Into The Separation and Synthesis of Psychic Opposites in Alchemy, 2nd Ed. London: Routledge, 1963.

Malachi, Tau. St. Mary Magdalene: The Gnostic Tradition of the Holy Bride. Woodbury, MN: Llewellyn, 2006.

Starbird, Margaret. `The Goddess in the Gospels: Reclaiming the Sacred Feminine. Rochester, Vermont: Bear & Co, 1998.

ON-LINE RESOURCES

Join our Facebook page at
https://www.facebook.com/ascendedmastersarah/

And our Facebook groups at
https://www.facebook.com/groups/sacredcircleofsarah/
https://www.facebook.com/groups/sarahshealingcircle/

More Sarah info
https://www.rachelgoodwin.dk/ascended-master-sarah/

Join Sarah's Wisdom School at
https://www.patreon.com/rachelgoodwin

Join this free Sarah 'Why Ascended Master Sarah now?!' class at
https://www.learnitlive.com/invite/class/12881/Why-Ascended-Master-Sarah-now

Who is Sarah, daughter of Jesus & the Magdalene and why is she here?
http://youtu.be/kgFbSa5bMNE

Channeling from Sarah. **'All is Well'** A message from Sarah through Rachel Goodwin.
https://youtu.be/PXJvg2unY5Y

Meditation with Sarah for the healing and purification of the Sea
http://youtu.be/KC0EIsZqpTE

Note From the Author: Reviews are gold to authors! If you've enjoyed this book, would you consider rating it and reviewing it on
www.amazon.com or https://www.amazon.co.uk

You can also email Rachel with your Sarah healing experiences from the techniques in this book at https://www.rachelgoodwin.dk/contact/

Thank you for reading this book and sharing this part of your journey with me!
Sarah blessings,
Rachel Goodwin.

ABOUT THE AUTHOR

Rachel Goodwin was born in a small town on the southern coast of England, and after being nominally educated at an all girls grammar school, left to try and find her way in the world. After unsuccessful attempts as a bank clerk, and then in the Royal Air Force, Rachel finally settled down as a mental health nurse, only to be launched onto a spiritual path after her mother died when Rachel was 26. In the years after this, Rachel learnt how to be a healer, channel, earth whisperer, priestess and Seiðr shamanic practitioner.

Rachel now lives in the town of Roskilde in Denmark, with her Danish husband and son, and can often be seen around the town happily talking to trees. She is available for individual and group healing walks around the springs, see more at:

<u>www.rachelgoodwin.dk</u>

Printed in Great Britain
by Amazon

84608780R00062